ABT

ACPL ITEM
DISCARDED

3 1833 02241 0747

LITZINGER, ROSANNE.
THE OLD WOMAN AND HER PIG

D0754560

**DO NOT REMOVE
CARDS FROM POCKET**

9R3

**ALLEN COUNTY PUBLIC LIBRARY
FORT WAYNE, INDIANA 46802**

You may return this book to any agency, branch,
or bookmobile of the Allen County Public Library.

DEMCO

The Old Woman
and Her Pig

HARCOURT BRACE JOVANOVICH, PUBLISHERS

SAN DIEGO   NEW YORK   LONDON

The Old Woman and Her Pig

AN OLD ENGLISH TALE

RETOLD AND ILLUSTRATED BY

Rosanne Litzinger

Allen County Public Library
900 Webster Street
PO Box 2270
Fort Wayne, IN 46801-2270

For my brother, Steve
Love, Sis

HBJ

Text copyright © 1993 by Harcourt Brace Jovanovich, Inc.
Illustrations copyright © 1993 by Rosanne Litzinger

All rights reserved. No part of this publication may
be reproduced or transmitted in any form or by any means, electronic or mechanical,
including photocopy, recording, or any information storage and retrieval system,
without permission in writing from the publisher.

Requests for permission to make copies of
any part of the work should be mailed to: Permissions Department,
Harcourt Brace Jovanovich, Publishers, 8th Floor, Orlando, Florida 32887.

Library of Congress Cataloging-in-Publication Data
Litzinger, Rosanne.
The old woman and her pig: an old English tale/retold and
illustrated by Rosanne Litzinger. — 1st ed.
p.   cm.
Summary: When her newly bought pig won't go over the stile,
an old woman tries to enlist the aid of some reluctant helpers so she
can get home that night.
ISBN 0-15-257802-1
[1. Folklore — England.]   I. Title.
PZ8.1.L926Ol   1993
398.2 — dc20   91-38227
[E]

First edition
A B C D E

The paintings in this book were done in
Luma watercolor dyes with pen-and-ink
and colored pencils on 140-lb. fine cold-press French watercolor paper.
The display type was set in Kleukens-Scriptura.
The text type was set in Centaur
by Thompson Type, San Diego, California.
Color separations by Bright Arts, Ltd., Singapore
Printed and bound by Tien Wah Press, Singapore
Production supervision by Warren Wallerstein and Ginger Boyer
Designed by Lisa Peters

An old woman was sweeping her house when she
found a crooked sixpence. "What shall I do with this sixpence?"
said she. "I know. I will go to market and buy a pretty little pig."

When she got to the market, the old woman picked out the prettiest little pig she could find. Then she gave the man her sixpence.

On her way home, the old woman came to a stile. But the piggy wouldn't go over it.

She looked around and saw a dog. So she said, "Dog! dog! nip pig; piggy won't jump over the stile; and I shan't get home tonight." But the dog wouldn't.

She looked a little more, and she saw a stick. So she said, "Stick! stick! poke dog; dog won't nip pig; piggy won't jump over the stile; and I shan't get home tonight." But the stick wouldn't.

She looked a little more, and she saw a fire. So she said, "Fire! fire! burn stick; stick won't poke dog; dog won't nip pig; piggy won't jump over the stile; and I shan't get home tonight." But the fire wouldn't.

She looked a little more, and she saw some water. So she said,
"Water! water! douse fire; fire won't burn stick; stick won't poke
dog; dog won't nip pig; piggy won't jump over the stile; and I
shan't get home tonight." But the water wouldn't.

She looked a little more, and she saw an ox. So she said, "Ox! ox! drink water; water won't douse fire; fire won't burn stick; stick won't poke dog; dog won't nip pig; piggy won't jump over the stile; and I shan't get home tonight." But the ox wouldn't.

She looked a little more, and she saw a farmer. So she said, "Farmer! farmer! yoke ox; ox won't drink water; water won't douse fire; fire won't burn stick; stick won't poke dog; dog won't nip pig; piggy won't jump over the stile; and I shan't get home tonight." But the farmer wouldn't.

She looked a little more, and she saw a rope. So she said, "Rope! rope! trip farmer; farmer won't yoke ox; ox won't drink water; water won't douse fire; fire won't burn stick; stick won't poke dog; dog won't nip pig; piggy won't jump over the stile; and I shan't get home tonight." But the rope wouldn't.

She looked a little more, and she saw a rat. So she said, "Rat! rat! gnaw rope; rope won't trip farmer; farmer won't yoke ox; ox won't drink water; water won't douse fire; fire won't burn stick; stick won't poke dog; dog won't nip pig; piggy won't jump over the stile; and I shan't get home tonight." But the rat wouldn't.

She looked a little more, and she saw a cat. So she said, "Cat! cat! chase rat; rat won't gnaw rope; rope won't trip farmer; farmer won't yoke ox; ox won't drink water; water won't douse fire; fire won't burn stick; stick won't poke dog; dog won't nip pig; piggy won't jump over the stile; and I shan't get home tonight."

And the cat said to her, "If you will go to yonder cow and fetch me a saucer of milk, I will chase the rat." So away went the old woman to the cow.

And the cow said to her, "If you will go to yonder haystack and fetch me a handful of hay, I'll give you the milk."

So away went the old woman to the haystack, and she brought back a handful of hay to the cow.

As soon as the cow had eaten the hay, she gave the old woman the milk; and the old woman took a saucer of milk to the cat.

As soon as the cat had lapped up the milk, the cat began to chase the rat . . .

the rat began to gnaw the rope . . .

the rope began to trip the farmer . . .

the farmer began to yoke the ox . . .

the ox began to drink the water . . .

the water began to douse the fire . . .

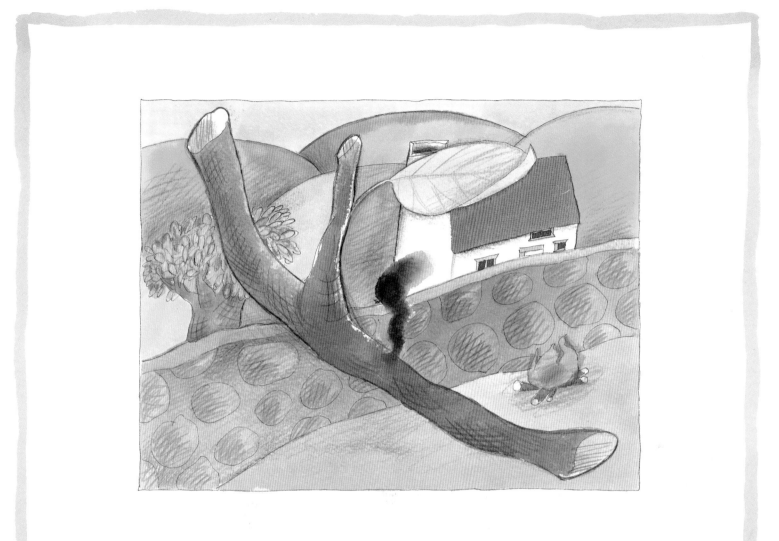

the fire began to burn the stick . . .

the stick began to poke the dog . . .

the dog began to nip the pig . . .

the piggy, in a fright, jumped over the stile . . .

and so the old woman got home that night.

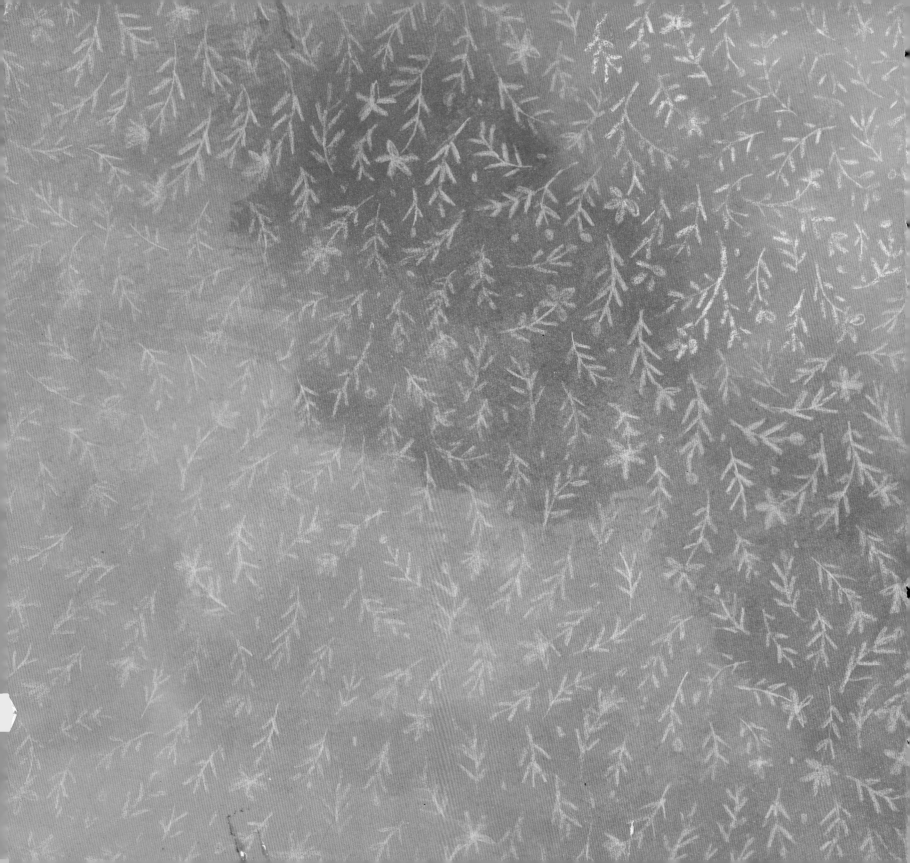